D1062537

Circulation: Please check for disc in back.

NO LONGER OWNED BY
PUBLIC LIBRARY

BLUE

By BLAKE HOENA
Illustrations by CONNAH BRECON
Music by DEAN JONES

CANTATA
LEARNING

WWW.CANTATALEARNING.COM

cd
E
535.6 HOE
6.18 dz

CANTATA
LEARNING

Published by Cantata Learning
1710 Roe Crest Drive
North Mankato, MN 56003
www.cantatalearning.com

Copyright © 2018 Cantata Learning

All rights reserved. No part of this publication may be reproduced
in any form without written permission from the publisher.

Library of Congress Cataloging-in-Publication Data
Names: Hoena, B.A., author. | Brecon, Connah, illustrations.
Title: Blue / by Blake Hoena ; illustrations by Connah Brecon ; music by
  Dean Jones.
Description: North Mankato, MN : Cantata Learning, [2018] | Series: Sing
  your colors!
Identifiers: LCCN 2017017501 (print) | LCCN 2017039445 (ebook) | ISBN
  9781684101481 (ebook) | ISBN 9781684101160 (hardcover : alk. paper) | ISBN
  9781684101955 (pbk. : alk. paper)
Subjects: LCSH: Blue--Juvenile literature. | Color--Juvenile literature.
Classification: LCC QC495.5 (ebook) | LCC QC495.5 .H638 2018 (print) | DDC
  535.6--dc23
LC record available at https://lccn.loc.gov/2017017501

Book design and art direction, Tim Palin Creative
Editorial direction, Kellie M. Hultgren
Music direction, Elizabeth Draper
Music arranged and produced by Dean Jones

Printed in the United States of America in North Mankato, Minnesota.
122017   0378CGS18

ACCESS THE MUSIC!

SCAN
CODE
WITH
MOBILE
APP

CANTATALEARNING.COM

3 6109 00542 5118

TIPS TO SUPPORT LITERACY AT HOME

WHY READING AND SINGING WITH YOUR CHILD IS SO IMPORTANT

Daily reading with your child leads to increased academic achievement. Music and songs, specifically rhyming songs, are a fun and easy way to build early literacy and language development. Music skills correlate significantly with both phonological awareness and reading development. Singing helps build vocabulary and speech development. And reading and appreciating music together is a wonderful way to strengthen your relationship.

READ AND SING EVERY DAY!

TIPS FOR USING CANTATA LEARNING BOOKS AND SONGS DURING YOUR DAILY STORY TIME

1. As you sing and read, point out the different words on the page that rhyme. Suggest other words that rhyme.

2. Memorize simple rhymes such as Itsy Bitsy Spider and sing them together. This encourages comprehension skills and early literacy skills.

3. Use the questions in the back of each book to guide your singing and storytelling.

4. Read the included sheet music with your child while you listen to the song. How do the music notes correlate to the words of the song?

5. Sing along on the go and at home. Access music by scanning the QR code on each Cantata book, or by using the included CD. You can also stream or download the music for free to your computer, smartphone, or mobile device.

Devoting time to daily reading shows that you are available for your child. Together, you are building language, literacy, and listening skills.

Have fun reading and singing!

Blue is a **primary color**. So are red and yellow. Primary colors can be mixed to make other colors. Mixing primary colors makes **secondary colors**, such as orange, green, and purple. But you cannot mix other colors to make the three primary colors. That is what makes them so special. Blue is also a **cool color** that makes us feel calm.

To see how the color blue fills our world, turn the page. Remember to sing along!

Oh, blue, blue,
I'm looking for you.

Got my blue jeans on,
and I'm singing a song.

Oh, blue, blue,
what do you do?

8

You **twitter** in the trees
and sway in the breeze.

9

Oh, blue, blue,

are you warm or cool?

10

You're the cool, cool color
of a flowing river.

Oh, blue, blue,
you're at the zoo,
sticking out your tongue
and splashing for fun.

13

Oh, blue, blue,
I hear you, too.

You're a funny tune
on a blue kazoo.

15

Oh, blue, blue,
what are you?

16

You're a primary color,
mixed to make others.

17

Oh, blue, blue,
what do you do?

You fill up the sky
and a blueberry pie.

THE LIFE OF PIE

Oh, blue, blue,
I'm looking for you.

Got my blue tennies on,
and I'm singing a song.

Oh, blue, blue,
yes, I'm looking for you!

21

SONG LYRICS
Blue

Oh, blue, blue,
I'm looking for you.

Got my blue jeans on,
and I'm singing a song.

Oh, blue, blue,
what do you do?

You twitter in the trees
and sway in the breeze.

Oh, blue, blue,
are you warm or cool?

You're the cool, cool color
of a flowing river.

Oh, blue, blue,
you're at the zoo,

sticking out your tongue
and splashing for fun.

Oh, blue, blue,
I hear you, too.

You're a funny tune
on a blue kazoo.

Oh, blue, blue,
what are you?

You're a primary color,
mixed to make others.

Oh, blue, blue,
what do you do?

You fill up the sky
and a blueberry pie.

Oh, blue, blue,
I'm looking for you.

Got my blue tennies on,
and I'm singing a song.

Oh, blue, blue,
yes, I'm looking for you!

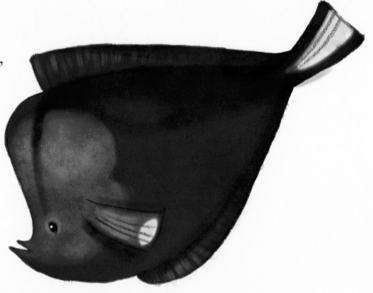

Blue

Folk
Dean Jones

Verse 1-4

1. Oh, blue, blue, I'm look-ing for you.   Got my blue jeans on, and I'm sing-ing a song.

Verse 2
Oh, blue, blue,
what do you do?
You twitter in the trees
and sway in the breeze.

Verse 3
Oh, blue, blue,
are you warm or cool?
You're the cool, cool color
of a flowing river.

Verse 4
Oh, blue, blue,
you're at the zoo,
sticking out your tongue
and splashing for fun.

Verse 5

5. Oh, blue, blue, I hear you, too.   You're a fun-ny tune   on a   blue   ka-zoo.

Verse 6-8

6. Oh, blue, blue, what are you?   You're a pri-ma-ry col-or,   mixed to make oth-ers.

Verse 7
Oh, blue, blue,
what do you do?
You fill up the sky
and a blueberry pie.

Verse 8
Oh, blue, blue,
I'm looking for you.
Got my blue tennies on,
and I'm singing a song.

Outro

Oh,   blue,   blue,   yes, I'm look-ing   for   you!

ACCESS THE MUSIC!

SCAN CODE WITH MOBILE APP

CANTATALEARNING.COM

GLOSSARY

cool color—a calm and soothing color that we see in nature, such as blues, purples, and greens

primary colors—the colors blue, red, and yellow, which can be mixed to make other colors

secondary colors—colors such as orange, green, and purple, which are made by mixing two primary colors

twitter—to make chirping sounds, like a bird

GUIDED READING ACTIVITIES

1. Looking back at the illustrations in this story, find these blue things: a bluebell (a type of flower), blue shoes, a bluebird, a blue tang fish, and a blue-tongued skink (a type of lizard). Are there any other blue things in the illustrations?

2. People sometimes connect colors to their emotions. What feeling or feelings does blue make you think of? Why?

3. Look around you. List all of the blue objects that you can see.

4. Grab your crayons and draw a picture of your favorite thing that is blue.

TO LEARN MORE

Adamson, Heather. *Blue*. Minneapolis: Bullfrog Books, 2014.

Cantillo, Oscar. *Blue Around Me*. New York: Cavendish Square, 2015.

Doering, Amanda. *Red*. North Mankato, MN: Cantata Learning, 2018.

Ghigna, Charles. *The Wonders of the Color Wheel*. North Mankato, MN: Capstone, 2014.